TEXAS

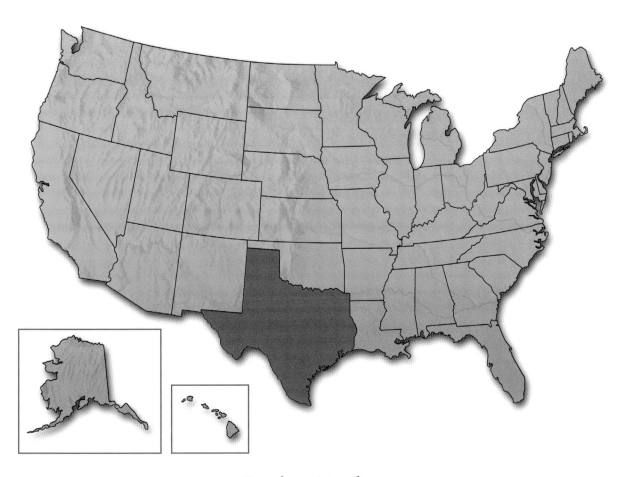

Janice Parker

Published by Weigl Publishers Inc.
123 South Broad Street, Box 227
Mankato, MN 56002
USA

Library of Congress Cataloging-in-Publication Data available upon request from the publisher. Fax: (507)388-2746 for the attention of the Publishing Records Department.

ISBN 1-930954-40-9

Printed in the United States of America
2 3 4 5 6 7 8 9 0   05 04 03

Editor
Rennay Craats
Design
Warren Clark
Cover Design
Terry Paulhus
Copy Editor
Heather Kissock
Layout
Derek Heck

Photograph Credits

Every reasonable effort has been made to trace ownership and to obtain permission to reprint copyright material. The publishers would be pleased to have any errors or omissions brought to their attention so that they may be corrected in subsequent printings.

Cover: Rodeo (Corel), Peppers (Corel); **Archive Photos:** page 7T-L, 7T-R (Imapress), 9R, 13T-R (R. Thompson), 19B-L, 21R (Russell Thompson), 24B-L, 24R, 26R (Reuters/Adrees A. Latif), 27L, 28T (Earl Young); **Corel Corporation:** page 7B-L, 16M, 16B; **Dallas Convention & Visitors Bureau:** pages 12B-L, 20, 26T-L; **EyeWire:** page 15R; **Lady Bird Johnson Wildflower Center:** page 4B-L (Texas State Department of Highways and Public Transportation); **Louisiana Office of Tourism:** page 24T-L; **PhotoDisc:** page 15L; **Planetware:** pages 3T-L, 3B-L, 7B-R, 12T-R, 20T-L, 20R, 23 B-L, 29T; **Texas Department of Transportation:** pages 3T-R (J. Griffis Smith), 4T-R (J. Griffis Smith), 4T-L (Kevin Stillman), 4B-R (Gay Shackelford), 5 T-L (Stan A. Williams), (J. Griffis Smith), 8B-L (J. Griffis Smith), 9T-L (Richard Reynolds), 9B-L (Richard Reynolds), 10T-L (Bill Reaves), 10R (J. Griffis Smith), 11T-L (Bill Reaves), 11B (Jack Lewis), 11R (Bill Reaves), 12T-L (Michael Amador), 12B-R (Richard Reynolds), 13T-L, 13M-L (J. Griffis Smith), 13B-R (Jack Lewis), 14T-L (Jack Lewis), 14B-L (Kevin Stillman), 14R (Jack Lewis), 21T-L (Stan A. Williams), 21M-L, 22T-L (Jack Lewis), 22B-L (Richard Reynolds), 22T-R (J. Griffis Smith), 22B-R (Kevin Stillman), 23T-R (Jack Lewis), 23BR (Jack Lewis), 25L (Richard Reynolds), 25R (Jack Lewis), 27T-R (Jack Lewis), 27BR (Bob Parvin), 28M (Richard Reynolds), 28B (Bill Reaves); **Texas Secretary of State;** page 6L; **The UT Institute of Texan Cultures at San Antonio:** pages 3B-R (No. 73-1557), 16L (No. 73-1533), 17T-L (No. 71-243, Courtesy of the Calleros Estate), 17B-L (No. 68-2291, Texas State Archives, No. 1458), 17R (No. 71-233, Courtesy of the Calleros Estate), 18T-L (73-1278), 18B-L (No. 70-559, University of Texas, Archives, Map Collection), 18R (No. 71-248, Courtesy of the Calleros Estate), 19T-L (No. 73-1557), 19R (No. 70-191, Texas State Capitol, Austin, Texas), 23T-L (No. 75-345); **Tom Stack & Associates:** pages 5B-L (Manfred Gottschalk), 29B (Jeff Foott); **Tyler Rose Garden:** pages 3M-R and 10M-L (Keith A. Mills); Woodson Research Center, Fondren Library, **Rice University:** page 26B-L.

CONTENTS

QUICK FACTS

Texas's motto is "friendship."

The state bird is the mockingbird. It is known for its lovely singing.

The state tree of Texas is the pecan tree.

Texas's state flower is the bluebonnet. It is loved by Texans, and many see it as a trademark much like the shamrock is to the Irish. The state's official tartan— a plaid cloth originating in Scotland—is the Texas Bluebonnet.

The first word in the third line of the state song, "Texas, Our Texas," had to be changed from "largest" to "boldest" after Alaska joined the Union.

The capital city of Texas is Austin.

INTRODUCTION

After Alaska, Texas is the largest state in size in the United States. For a short period of time, this large state was a nation on its own. It was called the Republic of Texas. That all changed on December 29, 1845, when Texas became the twenty-eighth state to join the Union.

Texas is as large as Ohio, Indiana, and all of the Middle Atlantic and New England states put together. It includes various regions including mountains, forests, deserts, plains, and a subtropical coast. Texas has a wealth of mineral resources. Few other states have such a wide variety of resources as Texas. In the twentieth century, Texas became the leading producer and refiner of oil in the United States.

Austin has a population of about 1.1 million people.

Getting There

Texas has two large international airports: Dallas–Fort Worth and George Bush Intercontinental in Houston. There are nonstop flights between Texas and Canada, Mexico, and countries in Asia, Europe, and Latin America. For land traffic within the United States, there are eight interstate highways running through Texas.

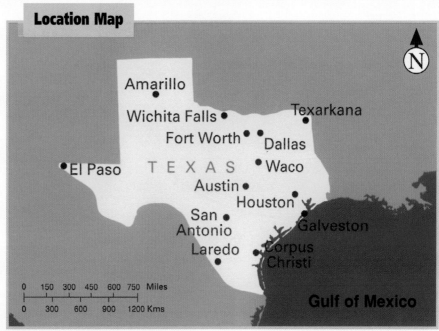

Location Map

Texas is in south-central United States. It is bordered on the east by Louisiana and Arkansas, and on the north by Oklahoma. New Mexico is on the west. The southeast border of Texas is on the Gulf of Mexico, and the Rio Grande River separates the state from Mexico on the southwest.

Texas has one of the largest networks of roads in the United States.

The Texas state seal was first created in 1936, and it was revised in 1839. It changed slightly from time to time until 1992, when it was standardized. The seal has a star with five points that is surrounded by olive and oak branches. The olive branch is a symbol of peace and the oak branch is one of strength. The words "The State of Texas" encircle the branches.

Of all the flags to fly over Texas, the Lone Star remains dear in Texans' hearts. Texas's nickname comes from the state flag, which has one star on a blue strip. Beside it, a banner of white sits atop a banner of red. Texas's flag was first used from 1836 to 1845 as the Republic of Texas's national flag. After joining the Union, this flag became the state flag. Just as the American flag, the flag of Texas has three colors: red, white, and blue. Red stands for bravery, white stands for purity, and blue stand for loyalty.

The olive and oak branches were added to the state seal in December 1839.

The state flag is the fourth of six national flags that represent Texas.

QUICK FACTS

The word *Texas* is an English version of a Hasinai Indian word meaning friends, or **allies.**

The armadillo is an official state mammal.

Texas has several official foods. Hot food is important enough to warrant two official peppers. The jalapeno is the official pepper and the chiltepin is the official pepper native to Texas.

The King Ranch in Texas is larger than the entire state of Rhode Island.

Texas's official insect is the monarch butterfly.

The large size and unique history of Texas have contributed to its culture. Ranches, herding cattle, rodeos, and gushing oil wells all play an important part in the Texas legend. Many people immediately imagine stetson hats and cowboy boots when they think of Texas. There is much more than this to the state. For more than 100 years, Texas was part of the Spanish Empire. Hispanic food, culture, and architecture all help create a special atmosphere in the state. These many unique characteristics make Texas stand apart from other states.

Cattle and horses were introduced to Texas by early Spanish explorers. Now they are a major symbol of the state.

LAND AND CLIMATE

Texas is made up of four major land regions. The Coastal Plain covers about 40 percent of the state. It includes the coastline and its beaches. The southern areas are warm and sunny.

Central Lowland summers are warm and dry. Winters can be cold and windy. The land in the Great Plains region is mostly flat and **barren**. Only a few trees and small shrubs live there. The winters can be very cold. Lastly, the Basin and Range region covers western Texas. This mountainous area is dry.

Texas has many different weather conditions. The coastal area has warm summers and mild winters. The mountain regions in the west have dry, warm days and cold nights. The rest of the region has hot summers and cold winters. Hurricanes can blow in the Coastal Plain region as well as the Gulf Coast.

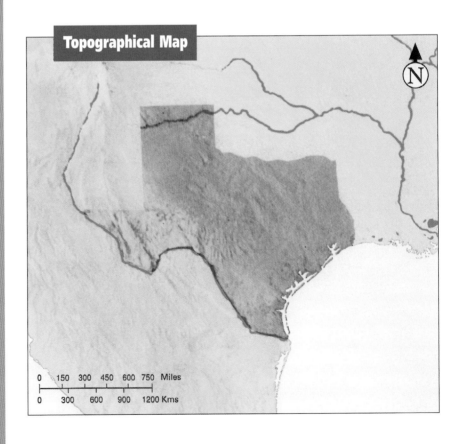

Topographical Map

NATURAL RESOURCES

Texas has many natural resources. Almost 10 percent of Texas is forest. Timber is an important **commercial** product. Some of the trees used for timber are pine, oak, elm, hickory, and magnolia. The good soil and rainfall in eastern Texas also provide the area with excellent farmland.

The state is especially rich in mineral resources. Texas has more petroleum reserves than any other state. Natural gas and coal are found in large quantities. Texas also produces helium, salt, sulphur, clay, cement, and talc.

Texas's location on the coast makes it a valuable **port** location for shipping and trading. The busiest port in the state is Port Arthur.

QUICK FACTS

The first oil well in Texas was drilled in 1866, and it began production in 1889. Texas has led the nation in oil production since 1928.

The deepest oil well drilled in Texas was 29,670 feet deep.

The Port of Corpus Christi is a major shipping location along the Gulf of Mexico.

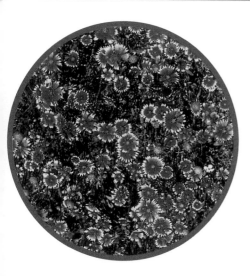

PLANTS AND ANIMALS

Texas is rich with fascinating animals and plant life. The woodland areas of Texas are home to pine and oak trees. Drier areas have mesquite, cactus, and sagebrush. The prairie regions have hundreds of different types of grasses.

Texas also houses more types of wildflowers than any other state. Bluebonnets, daisies, sunflowers, and asters are some of the most common flowers in the state. The official state plant of Texas is the prickly pear. The fruit of the prickly pear is called tunas, and it makes delicious jelly. The leaf pads, called nopales, are peeled and eaten as well.

The city of Tyler produces more roses than anywhere else in the United States. Although many citrus fruits are grown in Texas, the ruby red grapefruit is the only citrus fruit native to the area.

The prickly pear is a cactus people can eat. They have to watch out for the plant's sharp needles, which are actually its leaves.

Texas has more deer than any other state. Rabbits, foxes, raccoons, antelope, and armadillo are other Texas residents. More than one hundred species of snakes, including several poisonous types, live in Texas. The state also supports many types of birds, including mockingbirds, hummingbirds, roadrunners, and prairie chickens.

Whooping cranes spend their winters in the Aransas National Wildlife Refuge. At one time, there were only about fifteen whooping cranes left in the world. **Conservation** workers have bred the cranes and released them into the wild. Now there are as many as 300 cranes.

QUICK FACTS

The bog tree of Lamar in Goose Island State Park is 422 inches around. Scientists believe the tree is more than 1,000 years old.

The wingspan of whooping cranes can be as long as 7.5 feet.

Roadrunners can run up to 15 miles per hour.

Brazoria County has more species of birds than any other similar area in North America.

Texas is home to the largest bat colony in the world. Twenty million bats live in Bracken Cave, near San Antonio.

Jack rabbits have long hind legs and ears. They change from brownish-gray in the summer to white in the winter.

The pronghorn antelope is the only animal that sheds its horns every year.

TOURISM

About 40 million people a year visit Texas. Tourists spend more than $20 billion a year while in the Lone Star State. Many visitors come to experience the mountains and canyons in areas such as the Big Bend National Park and Guadalupe Mountains National Park.

The Gulf Coast has many beaches and **resorts**. Six Flags over Texas is an amusement park that has been made to look like the old west. Tourists flock to the Alamo, the historic site of the bloody battle during the Texan rebellion against Mexico in 1936. Davey Crockett's rifle is on display at the site.

Rodeos, barbecues, and festivals also draw people to Texas. The NASA Johnson Space Center offers guided tours to give people an idea of what space travel is like.

In 1969, the Johnson Space Center landed its first astronauts on the moon.

Guadalupe National Park has four of the highest peaks in Texas. It also has more than 60 miles of hiking and walking trails.

INDUSTRY

Since the discovery of oil in Texas in 1901, the petroleum industry has played an important role in the state's economy. Natural gas and coal are also important products that bring money to the state. Petroleum and natural gas are sent through pipelines from Texas to the rest of the country.

Manufacturing provides jobs for millions of Texans. Food, such as baked goods, flour, soft drinks, and meat products are all manufactured in Texas. High-technology companies build electronics equipment such as computers.

Texas makes more money from agriculture than any other state except California and, occasionally, Iowa. **Irrigation** helps grow crops such as cotton, wool, and grain.

Off-shore oil rigs drill oil from beneath the ocean floor.

Texas Longhorn cattle are very hardy animals. They have survived in Texas for more than 500 years.

GOODS AND SERVICES

The total value of all the goods and services produced in Texas is among the highest in the country. Agriculture is important in Texas. Cattle, grain, wheat, rice, hogs, cottonseed, pecans, and citrus fruits are just a few of the goods grown in the state. There are around 205,000 farms and ranches in the state. Some of the main crops include wheat, rice, grain, sorghum, and cotton lint.

Texas has more farmland than any other state. Cattle, cotton, and dairy products make the most money of all the Texas goods. Texas also has more sheep than any other state. The sheep are raised for wool. Texas is famous for its Angora goats, which produce **mohair**.

Texas also produces a large amount of the vegetables, watermelons, and honeydew melons eaten in the country. The state fruit, the red grapefruit, is grown in Lower Rio Grande area. Cotton, which was once just grown in eastern Texas, is now a major crop in the irrigated western areas of the High Plains. Grain sorghum is also grown in these areas.

Each angora goat produces 10 to 16 pounds of hair every year.

The oil industry accounted for much of Texas's economy for many years. The importance of oil is still strong but it has decreased with the introduction of other industries. These industries include food processing and aircraft manufacturing. Machinery and equipment production also brings a great deal of money into Texas.

Electronics are money-makers as well. Texas Instruments (TI) is a major producer of electronic goods and military communications systems. TI is only one of several companies manufacturing these goods in the state.

Chemicals are the leading manufactured goods in Texas. The amount of chemical production is second in the country only to New Jersey. Important products include benzene, fertilizers, and sulfuric acid.

QUICK FACTS

Texas is home to Dell and Compaq computers. Central Texas is frequently called the Silicon Valley of the South.

Texas produces more cattle, cotton, and cottonseed than any other state.

Other important goods and services in Texas include mining and fishing.

Manufacturing accounts for a great deal of Texas's goods. Goods, including refrigeration and construction equipment, are the leading manufactured goods made in Texas.

FIRST NATIONS

Native Americans have been traced to Texas from 10,000 to 15,000 years ago. These early people gathered fruits and nuts and hunted game, such as bison. A group called the mound builders made huts out of mud and wood. They also made pottery and stone tools.

By the beginning of the sixteenth century, several Native American groups had settled in Texas. Two groups, the Caddos and the Jumanos, created villages and farmed. They grew corn and vegetables and made homes out of grass and branches. The Caddos lived in the pine forests of eastern Texas. The Jumanos lived along the Rio Grande in the southwest.

The Karankawas were **nomads** who roamed along the Gulf Coast. They ate fish, small game, plants, and insects. The Apaches, who lived in the north, depended on bison for their food. They also built homes using buffalo bones and hides. The hides were used as blankets and clothing as well.

QUICK FACTS

The Hasinai people called the first European visitors *techas*. The Spanish pronounced the word *tejas* and used it to name the area.

Early peoples we call Basket Makers lived along the Pecos River in the Texas Panhandle. They built baskets and sandals from the leaves of plants.

The Attacapas, Coahuiltecans, Tonkawas, Hasinais, and Arkokisas also lived in the Gulf Coast area.

Bison are definitely wild animals. Their quick tempers make them very difficult to train in captivity.

EXPLORERS

The first explorers in Texas were from Spain. In 1519, Alonso Alvarez de Pineda mapped out the Gulf of Mexico coast and likely went inland to present-day Texas. In 1528, a ship of Spanish sailors, including Alvar Nunez Cabeza de Vaca, were shipwrecked off Texas's coast.

Cabeza de Vaca and three other explorers traveled for eight years through Texas and the southwest states until they reached a Spanish settlement in Mexico in 1536. They told stories of riches, including cities full of gold and jewels, that they had heard from the Native peoples.

In 1540, explorer Francisco de Coronado traveled from Mexico into the southwest states. He and his army found no sign of riches. In 1598, Juan de Oñate explored the area above the Rio Grande. After finding no riches either, Spain lost interest in the area for many years.

QUICK FACTS

In 1685, French explorer Sieur de La Salle intended to establish a settlement on the mouth of the Mississippi River. A storm on the Gulf of Mexico pushed him to Texas. He established a colony at Fort Saint Louis.

In 1996, the exact location of Fort Saint Louis was found. In 1995, one of La Salle's frigates was found in Matogorda Bay.

La Salle discovered the Mississippi River in 1683.

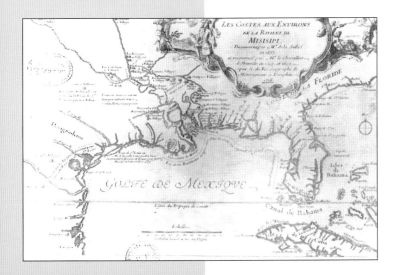

THE BUFFALO HUNT.

MISSIONARIES

In 1682, the Spanish returned to Texas and built a mission. They hoped to **convert** the Native people to **Christianity**. French explorer René-Robert Cavelier, also known as Sieur de La Salle, created a colony in southeast Texas in 1685. La Salle explored the land near the Mississippi River and claimed the area for France.

Within a few years, all of the French settlers at La Salle's colony had died from disease or been killed. The Spanish decided to take over the land before anyone else came to claim it.

For the next century, the Spanish built missions throughout Texas. Each settlement had a church and a military fort. Spanish priests tried to teach Christianity to the Native peoples. Soldiers protected the people living in the colony and the local Natives from attacks from other Native tribes. The Native peoples taught the Spanish how to catch game animals, preserve meat, and grow crops.

It was a priest's duty to the church to introduce Native peoples to Christianity.

QUICK FACTS

In the 1500s, there were about 300,000 Native peoples living in Texas.

MAP OF TEXAS AND ADJACENT REGIONS IN THE EIGHTEENTH CENTURY

By 1800, there were only 3,000 settlers and 1,000 soldiers in Texas.

Corpus Christi de la Isleta, established near El Paso in 1682, was the first Spanish mission in Texas.

EARLY SETTLERS

In 1820, the Spanish gave American Moses Austin permission to start an Anglo-American colony in Texas. Austin's son, Stephen, brought the first group of 300 families to the area in 1821. These families are called the "Old Three Hundred," and many of their descendants still live in Texas today.

The settlers moved to an area between the Colorado and Brazos rivers. The colony was called San Felipe de Austin. The first few years were difficult for the settlers. Their crops failed, and the Karankawa people killed many settlers.

Soon, people from the United States began to move to Texas. Over the next two decades, 20,000 more Anglo-American settlers arrived and brought 4,000 African-American slaves with them. These new settlers were not happy with the Mexican rule and fought to be an independent **republic** in 1836.

QUICK FACTS

Mexico had laws against slavery. Many of the early settlers to Texas broke these laws by bringing their slaves to the area.

Many Americans from the southern states moved to Texas during the nineteenth century. They often put up signs saying GTT (gone to Texas) before their journey.

Stephen Austin is often called the "Father of Texas."

Stephen Austin made many contributions to the settlement of Texas. He also held the position of Secretary of State for the Republic of Texas.

POPULATION

Although Texas once held many different groups of Native peoples, today there is just one reserve in the state. Members of the Alabama and Coushatta tribes still live in the area. Even though the French and Spanish were the first European settlers there, few Texans have Spanish or French **ancestry**. Most Texans are descended from people who came to the area from Mexico or from other areas in the United States.

Most Texans live in cities or towns. There are 1,186 cities in the state. Houston, the largest Texan city, is the fourth largest city in the United States. Texas has sixteen cities with populations over 100,000. The state also has hundreds of tiny towns, some with populations of fewer than fifty people.

Most of Texas's population lives in the northern part of the state.

A historic streetcar runs on Galveston's main street. The city is also known for its historic buildings, museums, and parks.

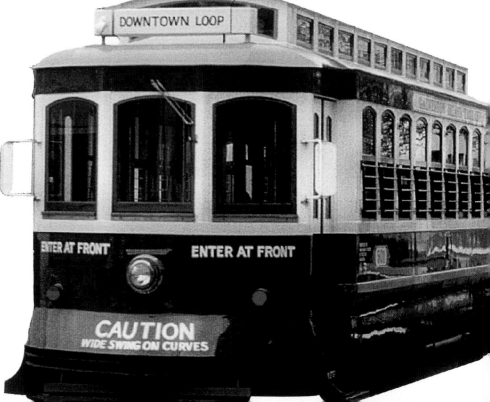

POLITICS AND GOVERNMENT

Texas is governed by a constitution adopted in 1876. The government is divided into three sections: legislative, executive, and judicial. The legislative branch includes the Senate and the House of Representatives, which make laws for Texas. There are 31 senators elected to four-year terms and 150 representatives elected to two-year terms in state government. They decide on issues including how to spend state money.

The governor is head of the executive branch and is also elected for a four-year term. The governor make sure that laws are carried out. The judicial branch includes the courts. The Supreme Court and the Court of Criminal Appeals are the state's highest courts.

Texas is divided into 254 counties. There are more than 1,000 cities and towns, each with its own local government. In the U.S. government, Texas has two seats in the Senate and thirty seats in Congress.

QUICK FACTS

Texas can split into five separate states under the terms of the 1845 treaty that made the Republic of Texas an American state.

Texas has been governed by several different countries including Spain, France, Mexico, the Republic of Texas, and the Confederate States.

President John F. Kennedy was assassinated in Dallas, Texas on November 22, 1963.

Texas had four earlier constitutions that had been adopted in 1845, 1861, 1866, and 1869.

George W. Bush, son of former President George Bush, became the forty-sixth governor of Texas in 1994.

Courthouses were among the first structures built in Texas. To early settlers they represented independent self-government and prosperity.

CULTURAL GROUPS

The Latino culture is found throughout Texas. Most of the Latinos in Texas have Mexican heritage. Many Mexican holidays are celebrated in Texas. Cinco de Mayo, on May 5, is celebrated with parades and festivals. September 16 marks the anniversary of Mexico's independence from Spain. The holiday is celebrated all over the state. Dia de los Muertos, Day of the Dead, falls on Halloween. It is a holiday in which the Mexican people remember their dead ancestors.

Latino music and Mexican food are very popular in Texas. Tex-Mex **cuisine**, which is a blend of South-Texan and Mexican food, is enjoyed around the country.

Texas hosts the National Barbecue Cook-off.

Cinco de Mayo is celebrated with music, dancing, and parades.

QUICK FACTS

Some examples of Tex-Mex foods are nachos, tacos, enchiladas, and fajitas.

Hot sauce is used like salt and pepper in Texas. One of the most popular kinds, Pace Picante Sauce, has been produced in San Antonio since 1947.

Chili is the official state dish of Texas.

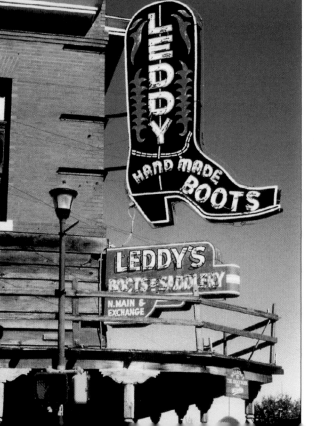

In the middle of the nineteenth century, cattle and horses were overrunning the Texas countryside. Cowboys would round up the animals and sell them in areas that needed them. Since then, the cowboy culture has flourished throughout Texas.

Cowboy fashion, which was originally designed to make the cowboys' work easier, has become fashionable with many people. Cowboys wear jeans without **rivets** on the back pockets, which could damage a saddle. They wear leather chaps to protect their legs from rain, brush, and cold. Cowboy hats protect their heads from sun, rain, or cold. Cowboy boots are designed to fit into the stirrups of a saddle. Cowboy foods, such as barbecued steak and beans, are an important part of Texas meal times. Annual rodeos also help keep the cowboy culture alive.

Cowboys and ranching are a distinct part of Texas's culture.

ARTS AND ENTERTAINMENT

Texas boasts several fascinating libraries and museums. The Texas State Library in Austin is the state's oldest library. It was established in 1839. The Witte Memorial Museum in San Antonio exhibits the state's wildlife, Native-American art, archeology, and costumes. There are also paintings and furniture from the days of early settlers. San Antonio is also home to the San Antonio Museum of Art, which displays various works of Native-American, Mexican, and Spanish colonial art.

Texas is also home to many different styles of music. Blues music has been played by freed slaves since the Civil War. Country and western music is also popular in Texas. Fiddle and guitar are often played in traditional country and western songs.

Stevie Ray Vaughan became a blues guitar legend. His death at thirty-five years old in an airplane crash devastated his devoted Texas fans.

Another type of music is a blend between the Mexican and Texas music influences. This music is sometimes called Tex-Mex or conjunto music. People from southeast Texas tap their toes to zydeco music, which originated with the Cajun or Creole people in Louisiana.

Many famous authors have come from Texas. Larry McMurtry, who wrote the novel *Lonesome Dove*, won the **Pulitzer Prize** for fiction in 1986. Texan Fred Gipson wrote *Old Yeller*, a popular book about a boy and his dog, in 1956.

Every October, a huge state fair is held in Dallas. This is the nation's largest state fair. Country and pop music artists play at the event. It also boasts the Texas Star, the tallest ferris wheel in the United States. It is 212 feet tall.

QUICK FACTS

Three million people a year attend the Dallas State Fair.

Austin is often called the live music capital of the world.

The first Dallas State Fair took place in 1886, drawing 14,000 people. Now the fair and its enormous ferris wheel are tourist attractions.

Texas hosts more than 500 festivals, fairs, and expositions every year. This is more than any other state.

There are around 620 newspapers in Texas. Around eighty of those are daily newspapers.

The television drama Dallas followed the lives and confrontations of oil-rich families in Texas. It was incredibly popular in more than 130 countries. The hit show ended its run in 1991, after thirteen years entertaining audiences.

Big Tex, a 52-foot tall cowboy, has welcomed visitors to the Dallas State Fair since 1952.

SPORTS

There are many professional sports teams in Texas. Baseball teams include the Houston Astros and Texas Rangers. The Dallas Cowboys football team has won the National Football League (NFL) championship five times.

Texans are also basketball crazy. It is home to three professional NBA basketball teams: the Dallas Mavericks, Houston Rockets, and San Antonio Spurs. It is also proud to claim the Houston Comets, a championship team in the Women's National Basketball Association (WNBA).

Texas sports teams have also found success in hockey. The Dallas Stars play in the National Hockey League (NHL). The team moved to Texas in 1993. Since then, it has taken the league by storm—it won the 1999 Stanley Cup championships.

The Rockets have been to the NBA finals four times.

QUICK FACTS

The Pecos Rodeo, held every year on July 4, was first held in 1883. It is the oldest rodeo in the United States.

Babe Didrikson Zaharias was one of the best female golfers of all time. She was born in Port Arthur in 1911.

Texas has many excellent college football teams.

The first football play-by-play on the radio took place in College Station in 1919. The game was between the University of Texas and the Agricultural and Mechanical College of Texas.

Rodeo is an important sport in Texas throughout the year. Professional rodeo began in the nineteenth century. Cowboys had contests to see who was the best at roping and riding. The best-known rodeo events are bullriding, bareback riding, and saddle bronc riding. In these events, a rider must stay on top of a bucking bull or horse for at least eight seconds. They hold on with just one hand.

Steer wrestling pits a cowboy and a horse against a steer running alongside them. The cowboy must move from the horse to the steer and then wrestle the steer to the ground by turning its horns. Calf roping events involve a rider lassoing a running calf with a rope. The cowboy then jumps off the horse and quickly ties up the calf's legs.

Bareback and bull riders do not ride with stirrups, reins, or even saddles. It is just them, the animal, and a rope.

Calf roping is traditionally used to round up calves for branding.

Brain Teasers

1 Texas is the only state to have the flags of six different nations fly over it. Which flags are they?

Answer: Spain, France, Mexico, Republic of Texas, Confederate States, and the United States

2 Which is the shortest river in the United States?

Answer: The Comal River in Texas is only 2.5 miles long. It is the shortest.

3 The Aransas Wildlife Refuge is the winter home of which endangered species?

Answer: Whooping crane

4 Almost all of the lakes in Texas were made by people. How many natural lakes are in the state?

Answer: One. Caddo Lake is the only natural lake in the state.

5

The first word spoken on the moon was the same as the name of a city in Texas. Which city was it?

Answer: Houston

6

Early settlers in Texas built homes made out of grass and dirt. Why?

Answer: The settlers often did not have enough time to build more sturdy houses before winter.

7

Texas entered the union in a different way than any other state. How?

Answer: Texas was the only state to enter the United States by treaty rather than being claimed through war or expansion.

8

What animals were called Hoover hogs?

Answer: Armadillos. During the Depression, people without enough money to buy food would eat armadillo instead of pork. Herbert Hoover was the president when the Depression began in 1929.

FOR MORE INFORMATION

Books

Bock, Judy and Rachel Kranz. *Scholastic Encyclopedia of the United States*. New York: Scholastic, 1997.

Bredeson, Carmen. *Texas: Celebrate the States*. New York: Benchmark Books, 1997.

Hicks, Roger. *The Big Book of America*. Philadelphia: Courage Books, 1994.

Stein, R. Conrad. *America the Beautiful: Texas*. Chicago: Children's Press, 1989.

Web sites

There are many great web sites on the Internet about Texas. Here are a few you can look at to find out more about this fascinating state.

State of Texas Web Site
http://www.state.tx.us/

Texas Best Online
http://www.texas-best.com/

Texas General Information
http://www.50states.com/texas.htm

Some web sites stay current longer than others. To find more Texas web sites, use you Internet search engines to look up such topics as "Texas," "Dallas State Fair," "rodeo," or any other topic you want to research.

GLOSSARY

allies: people who are friendly with one another or who have made an agreement on how to work together

ancestry: a person's descent or family background

barren: an area of land lacking any useful plant life

Christianity: the belief in the life and worship of Jesus Christ as the son of God

commercial: sold for profit

conservation: preservation or protection of natural resources

convert: to convince people to accept a new belief or religion

cuisine: style of preparing food

irrigation: using ditches, streams, or pipes to bring water to dry land

mohair: the long, silky hair of Angora goats that is used to make soft yarn

nomads: people with no fixed home who move from one place to another looking for food

population density: the number of people who live within a certain area of land

port: a harbor where ships dock

precipitation: water that falls from the sky. It can be in the form of rain, snow, sleet, hail, or mist.

Pulitzer Prize: the most important prize awarded for writing in the United States

republic: a country governed by an elected president and government

resorts: holiday locations people go to for relaxation and recreation

rivet: a metal bolt or pin

treaty: a formal agreement between two or more nations

urban: in or near a city or cities

INDEX